THE LEADER'S NEW CLOTHES

The

LEADER'S

NEW

CLOTHES

The Naked Truths

GARY HEIL *and* KARL MEINHARDT

ILLUSTRATIONS *by* TERRY JENKINS

You can fool the whole world down the pathway of years,

And get pats on the back as you pass,

But the final reward will be heartache and tears,

If you've cheated the man in the glass.

FROM *The Man in the Mirror,* FOUND WRITTEN ON
A WALL OF A PRISON CELL ON DEATH ROW.

CONTENTS

FOREWORD

How wonderful it is that nobody need wait a single moment before starting to improve the world.

ANNE FRANK

PAMELA LANDWIRTH *is president of Give Kids the World. She encourages and inspires her small staff and more than 1,800 volunteers—including Fortune 500 companies and family-owned businesses—to make a difference in the lives of children with life-threatening illnesses. Pamela also oversees the operations of the Give Kids the World Village and is responsible for all fund-raising, communications, and corporate alliances for the organization.*

Through 16 years with the Walt Disney World Company, Pamela has an extensive background in employee relations, resort operations management, and human resource development. As General Manager of Human Resource Development for Resort and Attraction Sales, Pamela was responsible for the training and the organizational development for more than 18,000 Walt Disney World cast members. Pamela currently serves on the Arnold Palmer Hospital Philanthropy Board, the Community Leadership Council, the Board of Directors for

America's Charities, and the Executive Advisory Board for Something MAAgic, a foundation established by American Airlines.

I find it challenging to describe the wonderfully varied experiences I have had with the Give Kids the World foundation. I continually have the unique opportunity to meet and get to know people from all walks of life, of all ages, and from many different professional backgrounds. During my time with Disney and with Give Kids the World, I have been repeatedly reminded how people, regardless of age and circumstance, love a good fairy tale or children's story. These stories take us all back to a time in our lives where our imaginations knew no bounds. On a child's level, the stories provide a world of fantasy, but for the older reader they teach a simple lesson by which to live.

Some of the most valuable management lessons come from fairy tales and children's books. If we take the time to revisit the Cheshire Cat, Pooh, Dr. Seuss, and others we just might find what we have been searching for—the blueprint for effective leadership. Although it would be difficult for me to single out one leader as the best example, it is easy for me to pinpoint the one quality that the leaders I most admire share: integrity. Other qualities can encourage and promote short-term results, but integrity is the only lasting means of motivating and inspiring a team long-term — a lesson *The Leader's New Clothes* helps us take from another classic children's tale, "The Emperor's New Clothes."

While many management books focus on how to make employees *feel* motivated, involved, and engaged, *The Leader's New Clothes* emphasizes creating an authentic environment where employees *are* motivated, involved, and engaged. An authentic environment is transparent and built on trust, and it also inspires a totally new level of commitment. Individuals are compelled to work with not only their hands, but also their hearts and their minds. They are engaged in discussions on core values and business issues, encouraged to provide honest feedback, and challenged to embrace a culture of open communication. When an authentic environment has been established and is functioning, concepts like accountability, responsibility, and quality become non-issues because there is a shared sense of reality regarding the goals and objectives at hand. The people in an authentic environment handle these concepts differently because they are all in agreement about who owns what task and what needs to be done. They have the information and the authority to finish the job. They are not afraid to take risks, to point out problems, and to share new ideas.

As I think back to the many management teams I have met and worked with over the years, I am reminded of several that resembled the Cladcom management team in *The Leader's New Clothes*. I remember them so well because I could feel the difference in these teams. They were inspired, creative, open to new ideas, and willing to provide honest feedback. Obviously, their working relationships were built on trust and integrity. Each person on the team knew he or she provided value to whatever tasks were required to meet the end goal. In short, they had established an authentic environment that engendered trust, integrity, value, and respect. My experience with such teams gave me the opportunity to witness authentic environments in action and provided real-life confirmation that such environments exist—they are not just fantasy.

Although *The Leader's New Clothes* is a fairy tale of sorts, in essence it is a "reality tale" that is timely and important because it envisions a completely different environment that is healthy, productive, and functional—an environment that comes only through authenticity. The blueprint for effective leadership just might lie in the "Naked Truths," and reading *The Leader's New Clothes* is the first step on your journey toward authentic leadership.

once upon a company

Once Upon

a Company

ot so long ago in a valley not so far away, there existed a company called ServiceProne that developed and sold software to midsized companies.

In the beginning, the company's product was cost-effective, simple, and easy to implement. As ServiceProne became more successful, the management team expanded ServiceProne's offerings to provide more complex solutions for larger businesses. While it seemed like the logical progression for the growth of the company, many of the company's current and prospective customers thought the new offerings were incomplete. As a result, sales declined, and customer service became more expensive and less effective.

Shortly thereafter, ServiceProne's problems were compounded by a sluggish economy, which caused sales to decline even further. The sales force continued to over-promise, and the company continued to under-deliver. The stock price plummeted. For the first time, ServiceProne fell on tough times. The company was in trouble.

At the end of the next quarter, the company posted a substantial loss, and the ServiceProne Board fired the CEO and much of the management team. The Board then retained a recruiting service that located an experienced CEO named Mark Hytop. It charged him with the responsibility of building an experienced management team, refocusing the company, and restoring it to profitability.

Mark began the process of reinvention. He started by hiring several executives he had worked with before. Then he mandated that ServiceProne be profitable by the first quarter of the new year.

In order to get a handle on costs, Mark began the process of downsizing the workforce. He implemented a rating system, fired employees rated in the bottom ten percent of the company, and announced that ServiceProne would continue to let the bottom ten percent go every year. He insisted that "A" players be hired and demanded "A plus" performance from every employee from the mailroom to the boardroom. In addition, he instituted an incentive compensation system for all managers based on their performance in a "360-Degree" review process. Mark demanded that the company be committed to quality improvement at all levels.

Shortly thereafter, processes were mapped, remapped, and streamlined. The most valuable customers were identified, and every effort was made to serve them reliably.

As Mark promised, the company achieved profitability by the end of the first quarter. Customers were more satisfied, and their complaints decreased. Productivity increased significantly, and the quality of the product was at an all-time high. Shareholders were happy, and the stock price was up. The results were so good that Mark appeared on the cover of several widely read business magazines. The articles highlighted the changes Mark brought to the company and traced the company's amazing path to profitability. Even employee morale was apparently improving — albeit slowly.

During the next several weeks, Mark grew restless. Sure, everything the business magazines had said about Mark was flattering (some of it was even true), but he knew that cost reduction was not a growth strategy and that ServiceProne must become more innovative to survive. To make the business grow fast enough for Wall Street, he had to change ServiceProne's products so that they would appeal to customers with more complex needs. Mark was aware that his predecessor had failed trying to reach the same goal, and he was determined not to repeat the same mistakes. He wanted to enlist an inspired effort from the employees of ServiceProne, many of whom were still cautious and distrustful of management.

Mark reasoned that to succeed in the future, ServiceProne managers would have to lead differently. They would again have to help reinvent the company. After much thought on the subject, he decided to schedule a meeting with the executive management team, or the "Team," as he liked to call them.

The Deep Carpet

The Deep Carpet

he day broke bright and shining as the sun bathed the ServiceProne office building in a warm spring light. The ServiceProne parking lot was full of cars as all the company employees got an early jump on the new workweek.

The ServiceProne Executive Conference Room was located on the top floor of the company building in a plush area that all ServiceProne employees referred to as the "Deep Carpet." Promptly at 8:00 AM, all the members of the Team were present with the exception of Mark.

Running a tad late, Mark strode through the conference door at 8:10 AM and greeted everyone with a big smile. "Happy Monday to you all!"

The executive team returned his greeting. Then, without any warning, Hap Camper, the COO, pulled the latest copy of *HotBoss* magazine out of his bag and asked Mark for an autograph. "Team," Hap said, "we have a star in our midst! Mark, would you be so kind as to sign my copy?"

The other members of the Team giggled. Then Bob Numbers, the CFO, announced, "Mark, we bought you a pair of sunglasses because your future is so bright! According to the article, you did it all by yourself!" The entire Team was laughing. Mark seemed to love the attention.

"Thank you all!" Mark said with a wry smile. "And don't worry. I don't get angry, I just get even."

"I'll bet," Hap chuckled. "Is that why we are here today? I noticed that the meeting did not have an agenda."

"No. I'll wait until you least expect it," Mark responded. Then Mark's expression became more serious. "I called this meeting because I am concerned that we are not as prepared to meet the challenges of the future as we need to be. Look, we have done a great job. We've come a long way and I am proud to be a part of this team." Mark's speech slowed to give emphasis to his words. "But I want to take a few minutes to reflect on the challenges we will face in the next few years. We spent so much time improving quality, listening to customers, and lowering costs that we simply haven't taken the time to make a plan to take the company to the next level."

Heads nodded in agreement around the table. "Well said, Mark," replied Hap. "I'm not even sure I can describe the next level. We've spent so much time trying to survive that I haven't given the next level much thought. Where do you think we should begin?"

"A few things are clear to me," said Mark. "One is that, in order for us to grow fast enough to satisfy Wall Street, we're going to have to change our products and our approach to deliver more complex solutions. That means we are going to have to change the way we do business. We are going to challenge every single person in the company to make a more significant contribution."

Healy Feely, the VP of Human Resources, seemed hesitant as he leaned back in his chair. "That's not going to be easy. Our employees have been through a lot. People are just now beginning to recover from the trauma of the last twelve months."

"It's *never* going to be easy. To be successful, we will have to ask people to change more in the future. I know they're tired, but . . ." Hap replied as he shrugged his shoulders.

"That's why I have often said that the best culture is a culture of 'celebrated discontent.' That's a culture in which we celebrate our accomplishments but act with a sense of urgency to meet the challenges of the future. We need people to stay engaged," interrupted Mark.

"Doesn't that describe our culture now?" asked Hap.

Mark paused for a second. "As I sit here today, I'm not sure that we have celebrated enough. We have not said 'thank you' enough. We have not taken enough time to feel good about what we have accomplished. But, at the same time, I'm not convinced we feel the urgency to improve and innovate."

Sitting up in his chair, Mark leaned forward and continued, "Our biggest challenge is going to be to lead more effectively. We need people to be excited about taking responsibility for creating a different future. We need to capture the hearts and minds of our employees."

"I agree, Mark," added Hap. "Leadership makes the difference. The executives that were fired before we came on board had very similar ideas but couldn't execute. They were smart people. They worked hard. But they couldn't get people to perform."

"We will have to do better! We have to be better than the previous management team, and we have to be better than we are today," declared Mark. "If we keep leading the way we have, we can't really expect a different result."

"So, what are we waiting for?" asked Healy.

"It's not that easy," Mark answered thoughtfully. "We can't behave differently until we start thinking differently. When we think about our future, we need to start thinking 'outside the box.' I have always been at my best when I have had to face new challenges."

All heads were nodding furiously. Agreement murmured throughout the group.

"Here is what I am proposing," continued Mark. "I want everyone in this room to think about how we can push ourselves outside of our comfort zones, think differently, and begin a process of transforming the way we lead the company. We need to have clear goals. We need to build an inspired team that is passionate about learning and improvement. We must change ourselves before expecting our teams to change. It will be harder than we think—are we ready?"

Jan Selling, the VP of Marketing, joined the conversation. "In my experience, when you are trying to think 'outside the box,' it helps to have someone who is not 'inside the box' to facilitate the discussion."

"I agree, Jan," replied Hap, chuckling at the box analogy. "I think we need assistance from someone who is not tainted by the box we live in. Anyone have a suggestion?"

Healy Feely spoke up. "Yeah, I know just the guy —Steve Daring. He has a great reputation for helping leadership teams think differently. I think we should schedule him for half a day to begin the dialogue."

"Uh ... instead of half a day, let's just try a couple of hours. It's difficult to get half a day on our calendars with so little notice," Mark said. The others were in full agreement.

Healy declared, "I'm excited by the leadership development opportunities that we have been discussing. However, I want to ensure that we eventually include all leaders in the process. For this program to be effective, we'll need participation at every level."

Hap was smiling when he interrupted Healy. "Program? I hate the word 'program.' Maybe it's just me, but every time I hear the word 'program,' I wonder if we're going to hire a mascot."

Mark was laughing, but his tone grew serious. "I am a little concerned about creating just another 'Team ServiceProne' or 'Customer First' program. The last regime had a 'Customer First' program where the customer was never first! Some of the same employees are still with us today, and they might get cynical."

Again, Hap interrupted, "Does anyone ever wonder why the names of these programs are exactly the opposite of what companies actually do? No wonder employees get cynical!"

Now Mark was adamant. "We are not going to do that! Let's not create a program until we are ready to make it happen. The last things we need are mascots, T-shirts, and high-school bands announcing what we don't do. Let me tell you right now, starting today we are going to think differently. Make no mistake about it. We are going to change starting right now!"

Randy Nano II, the CTO, jumped in. "Let's not have a program. Let's just say, 'The Future Begins Now!'"

Mark leaned back in his chair and thought briefly before responding. "I like that. Yes, that's what we'll call it. 'The Future Begins Now.' I like it."

Healy was eager to get things started. "Okay! I'll get in touch with Steve Daring. Let's set up a presentation to begin the program. Uh . . . I'm sorry. I mean the 'process.'"

Jan then asked Mark, "Who do you think should attend?"

"Let's get our managers and directors to attend. I really want to put all our 'wood-behind-the-arrow' on this. Let's get the dialogue started. Healy, set up a calendar event for Steve Daring next Wednesday in the Main Conference Room at 9:00 AM sharp. Make sure that everyone knows to be prompt!"

The Future Begins Now!

The Future

Begins Now!

I t came to pass that the ServiceProne Main Conference Room was nearly full with the company's top directors and managers. Wednesday had arrived, and the large clock in the room read 9:00 AM. The wide screen and podium were set up and ready, and "The Future Begins Now" was projected on the screen.

The managers seated in the conference room that morning had mixed emotions. Some were skeptical; some were excited by the possibilities. Most were curious to see what the Team was proposing.

21

At 9:15 AM, Mark entered the room and stepped up to the podium microphone. "May I have everyone's attention, please?" The room quieted immediately. "Before we begin our meeting, I'd like to take a moment to thank you for your efforts. ServiceProne is in a much better position today than it was twelve months ago. It hasn't been easy, but I'm not exaggerating when I tell you that you have saved the company. I am proud to be part of the ServiceProne team."

Vigorous applause filled the room. People were genuinely proud of what they had accomplished.

"As good as we are today, we need to be different tomorrow if we hope to be successful. This means, as the leadership team, we will need to lead differently in order to build more trust with our employees, to inspire more creative efforts, to innovate more quickly, and to serve more effectively.

"I don't have a specific road map to lead us into the future. However, I believe that we can be successful only if we all choose to participate fully and

THE FUTURE BEGINS NOW!

passionately. I hope you will join me and encourage every employee to take responsibility for helping the company grow."

The room was quiet. People were listening intently, but they did not seem energized by Mark's words. Mark quickly surveyed the faces in the crowd and continued.

"To begin our journey, I have asked Steve Daring to spend some time with us this morning to help put our leadership challenges in perspective and to challenge us to think differently. Please speak up and question the things we have done in the past. I know it's not easy to challenge past practices with your boss in the room. It's even more difficult considering where we have been in the last year. But we need your minds and hearts. We need your best thinking. We need your tough questions. And after that, we need to learn our way into the answers—together."

The audience remained silent but attentive.

"So, without further ado, I'd like to introduce Steve Daring. I am sure all of you read his bio. He has helped many leadership teams prepare for the future. We're fortunate to have him here today, and I'm looking forward to our discussion. I'm excited about what we can create together. Steve, thanks for being here today."

"Good morning, everyone," Steve said over the applause of the group as he stepped to the microphone.

"Good morning!" the audience replied.

"It is a privilege to be with you today. I have read of your recent accomplishments and am honored to be a part of your 'The Future Begins Now' initiative. I stand before you an unabashed fan. As we begin our time together, let me assure you that I don't have any easy answers to your challenges. If I believe anything after many years of studying businesses, I believe that every organization is as different as the people who work there and that every company must learn its own way into the future. I've also learned that it is harder to break from the past than most people think. We resist change in many ways—even without knowing we are resisting. I hope that we can be truthful and discuss our roles in creating the present and future of Service-Prone."

As Steve continued his introduction of the day's events, the back door of the conference room opened, and Mark's executive assistant poked her head in and signaled to both Mark and Hap. Mark and Hap quietly left the room.

Steve moved into his presentation. "To help us start the process, I would like to read an old tale. Though you may have read this story, I would bet you haven't read it the way you will read it today. I feel that there are many hidden issues in this story that are appropriate for leaders to consider. I ask you to listen and identify any issues that you believe are relevant to your experiences at ServiceProne.

"The story was written in 1837, by Hans Christian Andersen, and is entitled 'The Emperor's New Clothes.' How many of you know the story?"

Many people raised their hands, indicating that they indeed were familiar with it.

"When I ask people if they know the story, ninety percent of them remember that the Emperor was naked, but most don't remember the details. Bear with me, and listen closely. I believe the discussion of this story will be worth at least three graduate school credits in organizational behavior. Again, ask yourself, does this story apply to ServiceProne? And maybe more importantly ask, does this story apply to me?"

And then Steve read aloud.

THE EMPEROR'S NEW CLOTHES

HANS CHRISTIAN ANDERSEN

O*nce upon a time there lived a vain Emperor whose only worry in life was to dress in elegant clothes. He changed clothes almost every hour and loved to show them off to his people.*

Word of the Emperor's refined habits spread over his kingdom and beyond. Two scoundrels who had heard of the Emperor's vanity decided to take advantage of it. They introduced themselves at the gates of the palace with a scheme in mind.

They said, "We are two very good tailors, and after many years of research we have invented an extraordinary method to weave a cloth so light and fine that it looks invisible. As a matter of fact, it is invisible to anyone who is too stupid and incompetent to appreciate its quality."

The chief of the guards heard the scoundrels' strange story and sent for the Court Chamberlain. The Chamberlain notified the Prime Minister, who ran to the Emperor and disclosed the incredible news. The Emperor's curiosity got the better of him, and he decided to see the two scoundrels.

"Besides being invisible, your Highness, this cloth will be woven in colors and patterns created especially for you." The Emperor gave the two men a bag of gold coins in exchange for their promise to begin working on the fabric immediately.

At this point in the story, somewhere in the audience, a cell phone rang. Steve stopped his narration as many heads turned to see whose phone was ringing. Quickly the owner of the phone turned it off and apologized to the group for interrupting the story. Beeps could be heard around the room as many others turned off their cell phones and beepers.

Steve Daring continued:

"Just tell us what you need to get started, and we'll give it to you," said the Emperor. The two scoundrels asked for a loom, silk, and gold thread and then pretended to begin working. The Emperor thought he had spent his money quite well—in addition to getting a new, extraordinary suit, he would discover which of his subjects were ignorant and incompetent.

A few days later, he called the old and wise Prime Minister, who was considered by everyone as a man with common sense.

"Go and see how the work is proceeding," the Emperor told him, "and come back to let me know."

The Prime Minister was welcomed by the two scoundrels.

"We're almost finished, but we need a lot more gold thread. Here, Excellency! Admire the colors, feel the softness!" The old man bent over the loom and tried to see the fabric that was not there. He felt cold sweat on his forehead.

"I can't see anything," he thought. "If I see nothing, that means I'm stupid! Or, worse, incompetent!" If the Prime Minister admitted that he didn't see anything, he would be discharged from his office.

"What a marvelous fabric," he then said. "I'll certainly tell the Emperor." The two scoundrels rubbed their hands gleefully. They had almost made it. More thread was requested to finish the work.

Finally, the Emperor received the announcement that the two tailors had come to take all the measurements needed to sew his new suit.

"Come in," the Emperor ordered. Even as they bowed, the two scoundrels pretended to be holding a large roll of fabric.

"Here it is, your Highness, the result of our labor," the scoundrels said. "We have worked night and day but, at last, the most beautiful fabric in the world is ready for you. Look at the colors, and feel how fine it is." Of course, the Emperor did not see any colors and could not feel any cloth between his fingers. He panicked and felt like fainting. But luckily the throne was right behind him, and he sat down. But when he realized that no one could know that he did not see the fabric, he felt better. Nobody could find out he was stupid and incompetent. And the Emperor didn't know that everybody else around him thought and did the very same thing.

The farce continued as the two scoundrels had foreseen it. Once they had taken the measurements, the two began cutting the air with scissors while sewing with their needles an invisible cloth.

"Your Highness, you'll have to take off your clothes to try on your new ones." The two scoundrels draped the new clothes on him and then held up a mirror. The Emperor was embarrassed, but since none of his bystanders were, he felt relieved.

"Yes, this is a beautiful suit, and it looks very good on me," the Emperor said, trying to look comfortable. "You've done a fine job."

"Your Majesty," the Prime Minister said, "we have a request for you. The people have found out about this extraordinary fabric, and they are anxious to see you in your new suit." The Emperor was doubtful about showing himself naked to the people, but then he abandoned his fears. After all, no one would know about it except the ignorant and the incompetent.

"All right," he said. "I will grant the people this privilege." He summoned his carriage, and the ceremonial parade was formed.

A group of dignitaries walked at the very front of the procession and anxiously scrutinized the faces of the people in the street. All the people had gathered in the main square, pushing and shoving to get a better look. Applause welcomed the regal procession. Everyone wanted to know how stupid or incompetent his or her neighbor was, but, as the Emperor passed, a strange murmur rose from the crowd.

*Everyone said, loud enough for the others to hear,
"Look at the Emperor's new clothes. They're beautiful!"*

"What a marvelous train!"

*"And the colors! The colors of that beautiful fabric! I have never seen anything like it in my life!"
They all tried to conceal their disappointment at not
being able to see the clothes, and since nobody was
willing to admit to stupidity and incompetence, they
all behaved as the two scoundrels had predicted.*

*A child, however, who had no important job and
could only see things as his eyes showed them to him,
went up to the carriage.*

"The Emperor is naked," he said.

*"Fool!" his father reprimanded, running after
him. "Don't talk nonsense!" He grabbed his child
and took him away.*

But the boy's remark, which had been heard by the bystanders, was repeated over and over again until everyone cried, "The boy is right! The Emperor is naked! It's true!"

The Emperor realized that the people were right, but he could not admit to that. He thought it better to continue the procession under the illusion that anyone who couldn't see his clothes was either stupid or incompetent. And he stood stiffly on his carriage, while behind him a page held his imaginary mantle.

Steve gave the audience time to consider the relevance of the story. "So, what is this story telling us?" Steve asked. No one responded. Steve smiled.

As seconds passed, they seemed like minutes. Finally, someone from the back of the room quipped, "As Rome burned, Nero fiddled on?"

Steve asked, "What was that? Would you please repeat that?" But no one owned up to the original comment.

The room became uncomfortably quiet. In an attempt to lower the risk level, Steve ventured an option. "Would it make sense if we split into small groups to discuss the story?"

A low moan of disapproval rose from some of the audience. Eventually, Eric Lama, a front-line manager, raised his hand. Steve smiled. "Ah ... someone is about to take their finger out of the dike! Yes?" he asked as he acknowledged Eric's raised hand.

"Well, it seems to me that since this presentation is entitled 'The Future Begins Now,' it would be a great change *not* to split into groups but instead to give our responses in front of the entire group. I'd like to hear the opinions and reactions of everyone in the audience. I think that when we break into small groups, we miss much of what people have to say. And then, when we report our group's findings, the summaries rarely reflect the specifics of our thinking."

There was a mixed reaction to Eric's suggestion. Betty Cash, from Operations, disagreed. "I like the idea of groups. It makes it easier for some people to express themselves and refine their thoughts. More of us are comfortable with this method. It's what we know."

Mark reentered the room with Hap and heard the dialogue between Eric and Betty. He thought for a moment and said, "That's a great point, Betty. But since the purpose of this meeting is to think differently, I agree with Eric. I think we should all have the opportunity to express our reactions and insights to the entire group. Steve, does it work for you if we stay in one big group? I'd love to hear what the group has to say."

"Sure, Mark, let's begin. Eric, if you don't mind, I'd like to start with you."

Eric blushed. He stood up slowly and said, "I was afraid that I was volunteering!" The crowd laughed nervously. "Hmm ... well, I think we need more

THE FUTURE BEGINS NOW!

children here at ServiceProne. That's what I think."

Steve asked, "What do you mean, more children?"

"Well, in the story, everyone knew there was a problem. The Emperor knew it. His cabinet knew it. The crowd knew it. But it took a child, a person who doesn't understand the meaning of the word 'risk,' to open his mouth and tell it like it is. To be candid, I think we have too many grown-ups in our company and not enough children. Too many people are willing to agree with executive management when executive management is obviously wrong. I don't know if it's because they want to appear smart and likable. I don't know if they are afraid or if they don't want to disappoint. However, it's clear to me that they often censor what they say."

"Very good!" said Steve. "Thank you, Eric. So, you think ServiceProne needs more people who are not afraid to point out problems or to propose new ideas. But what is keeping people from speaking up?"

Susan Feelgood, a Customer Service manager, answered, "It's the risk."

At last, the dam of silence had been broken.

"The risk of what?" Steve smiled as if he had been here before.

Susan seemed nervous and hesitated for a moment. "Hmm ... I think it is the risk of being perceived as a non-team player or worse. Let's face it, I believe that being perceived as negative can be career-limiting. In the story, the Prime Minister, the Emperor's most trusted advisor, is faced with the reality that the 'magic cloth' is a farce. He is afraid to tell the Emperor the truth because he might be seen as stupid and incompetent. He is afraid he will lose his job."

A manager from Accounting stood up, looked at Susan, and said, "I agree with Susan. It can be risky to speak your mind, and I believe it's hurting us. If we don't share our ideas, we won't understand what is really happening in the organization."

Someone else from the audience quickly added, "And the farther you get away from the front line, the more distorted the information becomes."

"That's an interesting point! Would you mind expanding on that? What do you mean?" Steve asked.

"Well, let's say somebody shares information with their team. People may have misgivings, but they don't openly disagree. What we end up with is head-nodding instead of dialogue and innovative thinking. If we don't speak up, how are we supposed to have a common view of reality? How can we effectively work on our problems?"

Dave Beige, the Director of Facilities, stood up. "It may be worse than that. We may be rewarding people for wearing rose-colored glasses because we don't want to hear their criticisms."

Eric again took the initiative and offered, "I think Dave is right. I think that our unwillingness to listen turns people off. Let me give you an example. Just this week I saw an anonymous posting on our intranet web site that pointed out how many times I said the words 'process,' 'opportunity,' and 'challenge' in various team meetings. What is really frustrating is that my message to the team was lost. They were focused on word counting and not on what I was telling them. Either they were disillusioned about the value of their input, or they didn't see the value in what I was trying to communicate."

Al Facade, from Public Relations, disagreed. "A lot of realistic communication exists in this company. We have our regularly scheduled Total Quality Management meetings, employee reviews, and staff meetings, as well as monthly and weekly progress reports. We survey our customers regularly. We do a very good job of keeping in touch with what is going on in the company. We understand our customers. Just look at our stock price."

Eric, red-faced, interrupted and spoke directly to Al. "It's not that the meetings don't take place or that our stock price hasn't improved! It's what transpires or doesn't transpire in those meetings that concerns me. Are we hearing other people's opinions? Sure, we do surveys. But what are we doing with the information? I think not enough. Are we creating a culture for people to speak their minds openly? Or are we implicitly pressuring people to agree with us?"

Al replied, "I don't think you are giving us enough credit for what we're doing. I think you are being too negative. I think we do listen. We do act. I mean, there are only twenty-four hours in a day, so we can't do everything. I resent the implication that we don't listen effectively. How do you think that we got this far in the first place?"

Dan Abacus, from Accounting, stood up and said, "I agree with Al. We have worked hard to become a good company. It wasn't easy to implement our Total Quality program, but we persevered. We may not be doing enough, but we are doing a lot more than we used to. I personally try to listen to every point of view that is presented, and I resent the idea that we aren't listening."

Steve was happy to see that more people were engaging. He asked, "Are we getting so out of touch as leaders that we appear to be naked, just like the Emperor in the story?"

It was quiet for a moment. Then someone from the back of the room joked, "I hope not—you don't want to see me naked!" The audience broke out into nervous laughter.

Randy Nano II was still smiling as the audience's laughter subsided. He looked at Steve as he spoke. "I believe that the 'naked thing' is important. You see, I agree that fear is an issue. Apparently, the inability of some to speak their minds reduces our ability to address our problems. However, I think that the story raises a more fundamental issue. It goes to the meaning of the word 'naked.' It has to do with integrity."

"Isn't that what we were discussing?" asked Healy.

"Sort of," replied Randy thoughtfully. "But to me, the story lays out a simple but powerful lesson that is more about integrity and authenticity than just open communication."

Mark reacted quickly. "What are you getting at, Randy?"

"The Emperor loved clothes but ran around naked. He said one thing and did another. He didn't want to be seen as naked. To me, he wasn't authentic. And to make matters worse, when someone told him that he wasn't practicing his espoused values, he punished them."

Now Healy was shaking his head. "I'm beginning to get your point. The Emperor says dress is the most important thing but goes about in the exact opposite state and expects everyone in his kingdom to believe that he is true to his stated values. Is that your point?"

"Exactly!" responded Randy.

Steve was obviously pleased with the direction the dialogue was taking. "And how does this apply to business leaders?"

Now everyone in the room was engaged, and several voices spoke to answer the question. Finally, Betty's voice could be heard above the others. "In business, being naked would be like discounting customers or disrespecting employees. These behaviors are obviously unacceptable in business. You never hear a leader say that they don't care about customers or that they want to treat employees disrespectfully. Those would be career-limiting words. Just like no one wants to be naked at the head of a parade."

"Well, I might not agree that *no one* wants to lead a parade naked," added Chip Board, an IT director. "I can think of a few."

"Don't go there!" interrupted Bob Face from Business Development. "We can all think of somebody who might just like to be in that position!"

The room filled with laughter as a few fingers were pointed at specific people.

Randy raised his voice, trying to get the group to focus on the issue. "It may be a career-limiting move to say that you don't really care about customers and employees, but I have met plenty of leaders who don't really care. But, of course, they talk a different story."

"I agree," said Bob. "In my experience, many leaders talk a better game in these areas than they are willing to play. At other companies, I have worked for leaders who said they cared about the right issues but then turned around and did the opposite of what they said was important to them. In retrospect, I'm not sure they really cared about customers or employees. They said they were clothed. They said they cared. But when push came to shove, they were naked. They didn't care, or at least they didn't care enough. They had an integrity problem and didn't want to face it."

Now Mark seemed frustrated. He shook his head and pointed his finger at the group. "Is this lack of integrity present at ServiceProne? Is this a theoretical discussion, or are we talking about our company? Speak up! I want to know!"

Hap, sensing the stress level of the discussion increasing, stood up and said softly, "I'm sure that some people think that we don't consistently walk our talk. It is impossible to please everyone. But I think we do a better job than most."

Steve tried to diffuse the tension in the air. "'The Emperor's New Clothes' is a picture in which you can see different things depending on the way you view the picture. Your beliefs determine what you see in the story and ultimately what you will do as a result of reading it. I think this discussion is a good one."

"I do, too," Mark said. He took a moment and then stood up to address the audience. "I appreciate everyone's willingness to speak up. This is exactly the type of dialogue we need to have. But I must say that I am troubled by this discussion. If we are naked and pretending we are not, if we are not perceived as consistent in our willingness to hear feedback, if we don't have integrity, if we don't walk our talk—how can we ever expect people to follow us?" Mark raised his voice and said emphatically, "I hope we are authentic leaders. We need to get a handle on this issue now!"

After a second, Mark became quieter. "We simply need to have a better understanding of our culture. If employee distrust is widespread, then we need to understand why this distrust exists and deal with it immediately in a straightforward manner. And we better hold people accountable for getting their acts together."

Mark slowly walked to the front of the auditorium, obviously deep in thought. As he reached the podium, he said, "I would like each of you to hud-

47

dle with your departments to find out whether or not we are trusted by the employees. Do people think we care about what they have to say? Do they think we are in touch with their view of the world? Do we walk our talk? Are we naked pretending to be dressed? We need to know the answers to these questions. We need to know now!"

"That's a great idea, Mark," responded Healy. "How would you like this reported back to you?"

"I believe what Mark is asking," eagerly interjected Hap, "is for each of you to meet with your department as soon as possible. Report your findings to your department heads, and they in turn will relay their findings to us in next week's staff meeting."

Mark, nodding his head slowly, added, "Thank you, Hap. That is exactly what should happen. But I'd like to add that I don't want these meetings to turn into complaint sessions. I want people to suggest solutions to the problems they identify."

Steve took advantage of the lull in the discussion to close the meeting. "Let me just say that the first step in addressing any situation is getting all issues on the table. We have had only two hours together, and some interesting issues were presented. We have outlined the beginning of a process to deal with these issues. I think this is a pretty good first step, and I hope you agree with me. We all have to learn our way into the future. Different groups of people will solve the issues we discussed in different ways. There is no 'silver bullet.'

"When I look at 'The Emperor's New Clothes,' it reminds me that leaders need to be truthful in their approach and in their interactions. In my thirty years of consulting, I have seen many naked leaders who often pretend to be dressed when they are not. The best leaders I have seen are the ones who hear the feedback and then get dressed. The leaders who have the biggest problems are like the Emperor in the story. They are leaders who know that they are naked, but they continue to assert they are clothed."

Mark expressed his appreciation for Steve's insights. "Thanks, Steve. It's been a pleasure having you with us today. It seems like this discussion could have lasted all day. I am sorry we are out of time. But I can assure you, it is just the first of many discussions to come."

Mark then thanked the ServiceProne leaders for coming to the meeting. People filled out their evaluation forms and returned to work.

The meeting after the meeting

The meeting after the meeting

nd so it came to pass that the executive management team was once again in the Deep Carpet at 8:00 AM sharp. They waited patiently for Mark. Mark arrived at 8:05 AM and greeted the Team. "Good Monday to you all. How is everyone this morning?" Most of the group responded with "Great!" and "Wonderful!" Yet Healy responded with "Pretty good."

"Pretty good?" replied Mark, a bit astonished. "Just pretty good? How can that be? This is a great day! We have much to discuss. I know you are all busy, so we need to make this meeting short. I have a conference call at 8:30. Let's quickly review 'The Future Begins Now' dialogue that was held last week. What was everyone's impression? Are we on the right path?"

Most everyone agreed that Steve Daring was very good. The reviews from the group were positive, and the presentation received a high approval rating.

Healy thought for a moment and ventured his opinion. "I thought he was very good and entertaining. But I was a bit disappointed. He was great at getting people involved in the discussion, but when it came to proposing ideas about how to be better leaders, he didn't offer many concrete ideas."

Hap agreed. "It seemed a little too simple. Don't get me wrong, I liked the story. But ideas like 'Talk to your customers, employees, and partners' are things we are doing now. I guess the concept of being naked and pretending to be clothed was a good way to provoke a discussion. But I agree with Healy.

For the amount that we paid him, I expected more direction."

"I can't get over this nakedness thing. It has really been on my mind," Jan said as she shifted uncomfortably in her chair.

The team chuckled. They all seemed somewhat nervous at the possibility that they might be perceived as naked while pretending to be dressed.

Jan's comment triggered Mark's memory, and he asked, "Speaking of nakedness, how did your team meetings go? What did you hear from them?"

Healy was the first to offer his findings. "I have been asking around all parts of the company, and I must say that I didn't get widespread support for the concept that we are pretending to be something we are not. I found that people are grateful for their jobs and that they feel our leadership has saved the company."

Jan's experience was not quite as positive. "I didn't find as much harmony. I think they are grateful, but I think they feel that during these transitions they found management aloof and out of touch with their problems."

Hap smiled and said as though he were asking the obvious, "Isn't that always the case? I think most employees always think the leaders are out of touch. They simply don't understand how difficult it is to lead when substantial innovation is required."

"That may be true, Hap," replied Mark. "But if they think we are that out of touch with reality, how are we going to get them to follow us in the future? What did the rest of you find out?"

Randy explained that he took a slightly different approach. "I spent some time working in the call center the other day. Our customer service folks are getting a number of complaints. Clearly, both the service reps and the customers don't feel we are really in touch with customer problems."

Not one to be easily convinced of any discontent, Hap responded to Randy's observations. "The only customers who are calling are the ones who are complaining! Our customer satisfaction numbers are up. Eighty-eight percent of our customers tell us that they are satisfied. That's twice as good as it used to be. I don't think the people in the call center really understand the big picture. Maybe we need a program to articulate our priorities better and to give the call center an understanding of the types of challenges the company faces. They need to walk in our shoes for a while to understand how we make decisions."

Jan, slightly worried about the direction of the discussion, slowly shook her head. "I think we are all hinting at the same issue. It seems that our employees don't understand us. That is a little different from our original discussions focused on *our* need to change. We seem to be implying that they are the problem."

"Randy makes a great point," said Mark. "If we take a hard look at it, I think we would all agree that we have done very little to articulate our business problems to the front line. We must change the way we communicate. If they are to follow us, they must understand our business and our priorities. I agree with Jan. As we go forward, communication should be a primary focus. Anybody have any ideas on how we can make this happen? How do we get employees to understand the challenges facing the company?"

Jan suggested an idea that had been brewing in her mind since the presentation. "Maybe we need to look at great companies that have done a good job at listening to their workforce. I think we need a benchmark to learn from. We ought to visit a company that we think has the kind of leaders we aspire to be. Let's find a company that has wrestled with authenticity issues and that has experience in turnaround situations."

"I think that is a great idea, Jan," said Mark. "Any suggestions on who you think we should visit?"

Jan responded with a wide smile. "I'm glad you asked that question! I know Wilma True, the CEO over at Cladcom. She's a neighbor, and I often run into her at the monthly Valley Executives meetings. I think we are all aware of their reputation. They were in turnaround mode three or four years ago and now lead their industry. Their customers are apostles for what they do. Their stock price is strong. We have tried to poach some of their employees, but they won't leave the company. I think they'd be a great company to visit, and I think I can get us in there."

Mark was obviously pleased to see that Jan had been giving this some thought. "That's a good idea. I think before we hire more consultants, we should visit Cladcom to see firsthand what they are doing. I think all of the executives should go if you can arrange it. What does everyone else think?"

Everyone in the room voiced their agreement with the idea. All heads were nodding.

Hap was a bit more hesitant. "I think it would be great, but I have heard that they don't agree to meetings like the one we have described."

"I think that's true, but they might do it for us if I can convince Wilma that we are committed," Jan responded.

Nodding his head, Mark replied, "Let us know what they say. I am excited about this opportunity."

The meeting was adjourned, as they all had lots to do.

The Benchmark

The Benchmark

As luck would have it, there was one open visitor's space in the parking lot as the ServiceProne executive team pulled up to the Cladcom office building. It was Friday afternoon, and by the looks of the lot, the Cladcom employees were still hard at work as the weekend approached. Upon arriving at the front desk, the ServiceProne executive team was greeted by the Cladcom receptionist and escorted to the conference room.

The Cladcom CEO, Wilma True, walked into the room as the clock struck 2:00 PM. She greeted the ServiceProne execs. "Hello. It's a pleasure to have you visit us. Ever since Jan called me, I have been looking forward to meeting you. I have invited some of our team to attend the meeting. I wasn't sure exactly what you were looking for, but I hope we can be of service."

Mark responded by thanking Wilma for her time. "We appreciate the fact that you agreed to this meeting. I know you don't normally do this sort of thing."

"No, we don't," Wilma said. "We haven't found benchmarking very beneficial. Frankly, we have had more success stimulating ideas from inside our own company. We found that we hardly have time to implement our own creative ideas. In our experience, most of the ideas offered by our employees and customers are more relevant to our business. Have you found benchmarking helpful?"

"Well, to be honest, this is our first go at it," Mark replied, surprised by Wilma's candor.

"Maybe your experience will be better than ours," Wilma added, trying to be optimistic.

After all the introductions were made, Wilma seemed eager to move the discussion forward. "I have been intrigued by your turnaround. My sincerest congratulations! You must be very proud. What did you learn along the way?"

Mark smiled. "We learned a ton about how not to do things."

"Join the club! And your biggest mistake?" Wilma queried.

"We've spent so much time focusing on the survival of the company and the company's profitability that we have not spent enough time planning for the future," replied Mark.

"So, is this meeting part of your attempt to gain clarity about your future?" asked Wilma.

Mark thought for a moment, leaned forward, and said, "Absolutely. We've begun to set aside time to think about how we, as leaders of ServiceProne, are going to have to change the way we lead in order to effectively move the company to the next level. After spending some time talking about the issue, we decided a few weeks ago that we needed help to get us to think 'outside the box.' We had an interesting discussion about how we as leaders are perceived at different levels of the company. Clearly, we are not where we need to be. We know we need to grow the company and attract larger customers. We know we need to build more trust with our employees. We lost a lot of trust during the turnaround. We're hoping that as you share your experiences with us, we will become more creative in the way we address our challenges."

Clark Dotnett, the Cladcom CTO, asked, "Why us?"

Jan told Clark, "We admire what you have accomplished. You are not only good with customers, but the word on the street is that Cladcom is a great place to work. And, of course, the improvement in your stock price . . . we are fans."

"Thank you, that's very flattering," replied Wilma. "Let's begin with the idea that we will openly share information. Questions are great at any time. Agreed?"

As everyone voiced agreement, Jan leaned forward in her seat and smiled at Wilma. "Wilma, you and I have talked in the past about how the process of renewal began at Cladcom. It wasn't always like it is today, was it?"

Wilma rolled her eyes as she responded. "No! Just a few years ago, we were a very different company. In fact, I don't think we were very good. I'm proud of what we've done in the last few years, but it seems there is always so much more to do."

"What inspired you to be different? You just woke up one day and made a choice?" asked Mark with a huge grin on his face.

"No, of course not," Wilma responded. "But it makes us laugh when we think about what got us started. Every time I tell the story, I have to shake my head. You see, we hired a consultant to help us begin our leadership program. He seemed pretty sharp, but he did the oddest thing. He had us read the children's parable of 'The Emperor's New Clothes.' Do you know this story?"

The ServiceProne executives sat there with surprised looks on their faces and nodded their heads. "Yes, we are familiar with it," replied Hap with one eyebrow raised.

Wilma continued, "Well, at first we laughed and questioned its relevance. I mean, really, how could this story apply to us? We prided ourselves on the fact that honesty and integrity were part of our company's core values. They are listed on the little plastic cards we used to hand out. They had the mission statement on one side and the company's core values on the other. Every employee got a card. In retrospect, I'm not sure how many employees actually read the card or believed what was printed on it."

"So, you felt like the story didn't apply to you?" Healy asked.

"Well, we might have thought that at first. But the more we discussed it and the more we thought about it, the more that we came to realize the story was relevant. Like the Emperor in the story, we were often naked but acted as if we were dressed. Unfortunately, we'd say one thing and do another. And when people called us on our inconsistency, we often reacted harshly. It wasn't easy to be a *child* in our company."

"You heard the story and reached that conclusion?" Hap asked with a hint of astonishment in his voice.

"Don't get me wrong," Wilma said as she shook her head. "This realization wasn't a two-minute exercise. The dialogue that followed that story took weeks and continues to this day. We didn't want to believe that we talked a better game than we played. We prided ourselves on our openness and honesty. It wasn't until Clark stood up and told us of his past experiences that we began to consider seriously how much our stated values differed from the values that we actually lived day to day. Clark, tell them what you told us."

Clark settled back in his chair, and a serious expression crossed his face when he told his story. "I told the group how I lost my last job. I was, for lack of a better term, 'resigned.' You see, I wouldn't agree to a set of projections that, in my opinion, were misleading and unrealistic. I didn't feel it was right to mislead the Board with projections that I knew we couldn't achieve. It wasn't a matter of setting aggressive goals. I'm all for that if they are realistic. But my boss wanted to use these projections to tell the Board what revenue we could expect from customers. When I wouldn't agree to his numbers, I was 'resigned.' I've talked to my successor, and I can assure you that he quickly learned what was expected of him in that company—and it wasn't what was listed on their core values statement."

A moment of uneasy silence arose until Wilma spoke. "After hearing Clark's story, I remember thinking to myself, 'That wouldn't happen here.' To be truthful, I can't remember much of the rest of the discussion that day because I kept asking myself, 'Could it happen here?' I don't think I ever came to a solid conclusion that afternoon. What I do remember, however, is how I didn't sleep that night. I kept wondering if Cladcom's culture was consistent with its values. I mean, I can be pretty tough sometimes, so I wondered if Clark's experience could happen here. Could I be saying that our values are important and then, unintentionally, acting in ways that confuse and frustrate people? To use the vocabulary of the story, I kept asking myself if I was really naked—pretending to be clothed."

Jan, empathizing with Wilma's uneasiness about the concept of nakedness, asked, "So, what did you do?"

"I did what I usually do when I have problems I can't resolve. I called my mentor, whom I have worked for a number of times in my career. I read her the story of 'The Emperor's New Clothes' and asked her if she thought I might be acting less than 'authentically' in my present position."

Jan sat up quickly. "What did she say?"

"Well, her answer surprised me. She told me that it was not only possible, but it was also likely that I was less than authentic. In fact, she added that in nearly all organizations political behavior is rewarded more than authentic behavior. She suggested a test and said it would be simple. She asked me to look at my calendar and compare it to my stated priorities. If my priorities are not readily apparent on my calendar, then they are really not my priorities. She told me that this was not the only test for authenticity, but usually this test alone demonstrates potential inconsistencies. And you know what I found when I did the comparison?"

"They didn't match up, did they?" asked Mark.

"No!" replied Wilma. "It was a hard lesson. Integrity has always been important to me. I thought that I had continually 'walked my talk.' Now I was faced with clear evidence to the contrary."

Jan nodded her head. "If you asked any of us to take the same test, I bet we'd all have similar results."

Hap thought for a moment. "I'm not sure I agree. I think most of our calendars are consistent with the critical business issues we face. Can you give me an example of what you are describing?"

"I can give you lots of examples," responded Wilma, puzzled by Hap's comments. "I have often talked about how important it is for executives to talk with new employees. But I had stopped attending new-hire indoctrination meetings. I also talked about the need to get closer to our customers, but precious few customer meetings were on my calendar. I was passionate about the need for leadership development. Yet I couldn't find time on my calendar to participate actively in the process. Heck, when things got tough a few years ago, I canceled the funds necessary to continue our leadership development program! I think you get the point."

"Okay, so what did you do about this?" asked Mark, seeming to grow more uncomfortable by the second.

"Well, I have to admit that I struggled with our apparent lack of authenticity for some time. But in the end, I knew I had to discuss it with the Cladcom executive team."

The Cladcom VP of Sales, Stan Target, fidgeted in his chair as he spoke. "Man, I'll never forget that meeting! That's when she came to us and asked us to choose. Wilma told us that she felt she was not being authentic, and she guessed that we were probably in the same boat. She had each of us do the 'Calendar Check.' She wondered whether any of us had ever consistently 'walked our talk' in the way she was thinking about it. I remember that meeting as the ultimate 'Come to Wilma' meeting."

"That was without a doubt the toughest meeting of my career!" chimed in Sharon Clockwork, the Cladcom COO. "But you know what? It was also the most rewarding meeting I have ever attended. Once the discussion began, we identified many examples where we were not being authentic. It became clear. We were naked and didn't want to admit it. It was amazing! At one point, I think it was Clark who asked if anyone else in the room felt uneasy taking bonuses last year. We downsized a lot of people. I'll never forget the facial expressions in the room."

Wilma continued her story. "So we spent the next couple of weeks asking 'Just how naked are we?' "

Mark was impressed by the candor and the enthusiasm of the Cladcom team. He could see that this team was really different. "And what did you find?" he asked.

Wilma took a moment to find the right words. "We found that we were acting so loudly that you could hardly hear our words. As a team we felt we had to make a decision. We all felt in the pits of our stomachs that we were about to choose to lead in a way that we had never led before. To be truthful, we felt like Butch Cassidy and the Sundance Kid jumping off that cliff without knowing whether we could survive the fall. That's how our transformation began. And as it progressed, it became more and more rewarding. I must tell you that although it was difficult at times, we've never had more fun. We've never been more productive. And we've never been more proud of what we have accomplished."

Obviously, Mark did not want the dialogue to end. "Please continue! How did this progress? What did you learn?"

"I cannot overestimate the power of committing to the truth," Wilma answered with slow, deliberate words to stress their importance. "Consistently telling the truth is one of the most difficult things I have ever done. It seems like it should be easy, but it's not. I can tell you that being honest is the secret to learning and innovation. It permits us to stop do-ing silly things faster. Think about your past expe-riences for a second. Have you ever wondered why your former bosses continued on a path that every-one knew wouldn't work? If people were honest with them and told them how silly the effort was, they might have stopped the insanity. How many times in our business careers have we been re-warded for being less than candid?"

"Of course, we've all been there," replied Mark. There was general agreement among the entire group and clear discomfort among the Service-Prone team.

The excitement on Clark's face was apparent. The passion in his voice sent a message as impor-tant as his words. "We decided that we couldn't ef-fectively lead if we continued to spin the truth! We were acting in ways that confused people about our priorities, and when they challenged our actions we ... I'm embarrassed to say ... we often made it punishing."

Randy Nano II smirked as he shook his head. "I'm sure *that* made it easy to speak up!"

Striking a more serious tone, Wilma continued, "Yes, and it made it tough for us to understand how people felt about the way we were leading. We didn't feel good when they told us we were ineffective and inhibiting their ability to do their jobs. We felt even worse when we realized that what they were really telling us is that we were inauthentic. But once we listened and accepted the feedback, we knew that we had to change. There was no going back."

Sharon spoke up. "I'm not sure whether we really believed that we were being authentic or whether we were just hoping that no one would notice that we were not acting authentically. Or, in the words of the story, we were hoping that they would not notice that we were naked. But when we finally began to value the perception of others, we began to understand how our view of the world did not fit the reality of the people we were attempting to lead."

Stan Target added his insight. "I can't emphasize this enough! We found that it is really important that *everyone* see things as they are and not the way they wish they were. People must believe that you really want to hear what they have to say. It's the only way a team can share a view of reality."

Wilma nodded her head in agreement. "That is very important! You see, first you must understand that there is no reality—only perceived reality—and everyone has different perceptions based on their experiences. Then you start to understand that by having diverse views of what is happening, you get to see things differently. You get a more complete view of the way you are leading and the challenges you face. We realized we were stifling information flow, especially negative information. We were saying things like, 'Don't bring me a problem without a solution.' How bad was that? We told people that they should ask questions only if they had the answer. We couldn't have found a better way to stifle critical thinking if that had been our goal. And this was just the tip of the iceberg. We did many subtle things that inhibited our ability to get a realistic picture of the world around us. It seems silly now, but at the time, we thought we were progressive leaders.

"So we implemented a company-wide education process to explain our business challenges past, present, and future. Once our employees understood more about the challenges that the company faced, the more freely they expressed their ideas. Predictably, the more educated people were, the more insightful their comments became. We didn't try to make them *feel* involved in the improvement process. They *were* involved. They knew we were listening, and they didn't hesitate to let us know what they thought."

Hap interjected incredulously, "But I'm sure some of what you heard had to be uneducated nonsense!"

"Well, some of it was. Heck, much of it was," replied Clark. "But it was how people felt, and that's what was important to us. If they had nonsensical responses, it was generally not because they were not smart. It was because we had not given them a context for understanding the business. But you know, Hap, we found that a little naiveté was a great asset. So many times we think we know what won't work because we have been here for a long time. And, oddly enough, some of the comments and ideas that helped us learn the most were the ones that seemed the most outrageous. It made us stop and look at them with a creative eye and ask ourselves, 'Well, why not? Why shouldn't we try that? Why wouldn't that work?' "

"We even took it a step further," added Wilma. "We started to celebrate the person in our company who contributed the most creative idea each week. We called it the Weird Idea Award. I know that sounds crazy, but once we let people know that we valued what they had to say, we got more ideas than we could handle."

Clark was obviously enjoying the direction of the conversation. "That is so true. At first the feedback we solicited was about our nakedness issue —about our leadership effectiveness. But what we found was that by opening a dialogue with the rest of the company, we began learning faster and innovating more than we ever had before. People were really engaged."

"It must have been a great problem to have," suggested Jan.

"It *is* a great problem to have! I can tell you that it sure changed my life and the life of all our leaders and employees. But we didn't stop with the employees. We took the same approach with our customers. Instead of customer surveys, which now seem like old data to me, we started having conversations with our customers. We invited them to participate in our Weird Idea Program."

Stan, always in favor of more revenue, added with a huge grin, "And we learned the hard way that you have to be careful when you invite today's customers to a Weird Idea Party. Let me tell you, we got a few *really* weird ideas. But some of those ideas fundamentally changed our relationship with those customers. And the loyalty that evolved led to more sales and more profits. What a concept, eh?"

After a short pause in the conversation, Mark asked, "You got all that out of this speaker's presentation and 'The Emperor's New Clothes'?" More than a hint of amazement was in his question.

Wilma looked right at Mark and replied, "You know, Mark, I have to admit that the presentation got us started on the path we are now on. I think I mentioned earlier that we now look back on it and are amused and a little embarrassed by it. But all the improvements we've made in the last few years have stemmed from the one element Steve Daring's presentation emphasized."

"And that is?" asked Mark.

"*Authenticity*," Wilma told him in a reverent voice. "It is the key to building the credibility that enables us to touch the hearts, as well as the minds, of the people who have allowed us to lead. We found that when we became authentic, everything got easier because the relationships in our company changed. They became more fulfilling and more effective."

"You make it sound so simple!" sighed Jan as she leaned back and shook her head.

Wilma smiled at Jan. She knew exactly how Jan felt. "It is a simple concept, really. But I am here to tell you that while the concept is simple, its implementation is anything but simple. To be authentic is a choice that has to be made by *every* member of the leadership team. Employees and customers can easily spot when our actions and words are inconsistent."

"Wilma, the words seem to come so easily for you—" marveled Mark.

Before Mark could finish his thought, Wilma interrupted him. "As I just said, it wasn't simple. When I said it wasn't simple, what I really meant was that it was very difficult. No one can tell you how difficult it is. You would only understand by trying to do it. But maybe I can give you a hint of what it was like for me by describing just a few of the challenges I faced.

"For instance, a few years ago I instituted a policy that we would annually lay off people whose performance ranked in the bottom ten percent of our workforce. This practice is still popular in many companies. When I was asked to explain how this policy was consistent with our core values of fairness and respect, I had a problem. I could rationalize how it might work in the first year if we had not been holding people accountable. But in subsequent years you begin to cut muscle from that organization. And if you institute this policy across the board, as I did, you force valuable players off effective teams.

"And I have always been an advocate of teamwork. In fact, I can give one hell of a teamwork speech. But I had to face the fact that throughout my entire career I have perpetuated human resource practices that made effective teamwork nearly impossible. I mean, let's face it, most performance appraisal and incentive compensation practices are designed to be internally competitive. We had to reinvent our human resource practices before we had a proven alternative. It wasn't easy, and it took a lot of time and effort.

"It was really hard for me to meet with a group of employees after we had downsized the company and have them tell me that our management team purposely and unfairly laid off talented, hardworking employees simply because they weren't popular. At first I argued that that could never happen in our company, but after I investigated the circumstances, I found that these employee complaints were true. I had to admit that I didn't listen in time to prevent these acts from occurring.

"And you know, I can still remember saying at meetings that the reason Cladcom existed was to increase shareholder value. But as we began to create more dialogue with employees, we found that, although they agreed that shareholder value was important, it wasn't the primary reason they came to work. They came to work because they wanted to build great products, to serve customers, to build a great company, and to reach their potential. It was different for each person. But *nobody* told me that the primary reason they came to Cladcom was to create more wealth for people they didn't know. I heard an analogy that I've adopted. *Food is important. People need to eat, but they don't live to eat. Shareholder value is important, but it is not the reason we exist.*

"I could go on, but I will spare you the details. To be authentic is hard work. The quickest way to fail is to underestimate the challenge."

As Wilma finished her thoughts, the room was silent. Everyone in the room was in some way touched by her comments.

After a few minutes, Mark glanced at the clock at the end of the conference room and frowned. "I hate to say this, but our time is up. I really wish we could continue this conversation. I want to thank you for meeting with us."

Wilma replied, "You are welcome! It has been our pleasure."

Mark seemed hesitant and turned to Wilma. "Before we go, I have to admit something to you. I have to tell you that we hired the same consultant, Steve Daring, and heard the same children's story, 'The Emperor's New Clothes.' The interesting thing is that I wasn't ready for his message. I'm a bit embarrassed to admit this, but I obviously missed the point. But if I am going to be committed to authenticity, then I think admitting this is a good first step!"

"Well done!" replied Wilma excitedly. "The first step is always the hardest. I'm glad to see you make it. And to help you make the second step, we have parting gifts for all of you. It was Clark's idea, and I was a bit hesitant at first because I wasn't sure how you'd respond to our meeting. But I think you're ready for them. Clark?"

Clark reached under the table and pulled out a box. As he opened the box, he smiled. "These were created as a result of our Weird Idea Program. They helped us. We hope they will help you on your journey to authenticity." Just as he finished, Clark held up a plain white T-shirt. On it was printed in big black letters: "AM I NAKED?"

"Before you go, let me give you one word of advice about these shirts," added Wilma with a very serious expression. "Don't wear them unless you are ready to answer the question!"

The Naked Truths

The Naked Truths

Once again, Monday arrived as the sun shone with the promise of a new work-week at ServiceProne. The members of the Team were assembled in the ServiceProne Executive Conference Room, habitually expecting a few minutes of downtime until Mark arrived to start the meeting. Much to their surprise, however, on this day, Mark entered the room at 8:00 AM sharp wearing the "AM I NAKED?" T-shirt Wilma had given him.

The room fell quiet as Mark entered. The Team was curious to see what Mark was thinking.

"Hello, everyone. I trust you had a great weekend."

The Team was unusually quiet. No one in the group made eye contact with Mark until Hap broke the silence. "I had a great weekend, and it was a thoughtful one. I couldn't stop thinking about our meeting at Cladcom." Hap then pointed to Mark's T-shirt. "It seems you spent some time thinking about the same issues."

Mark was smiling as Hap spoke, nodding his head thoughtfully while he responded to Hap's observation. "I had a few sleepless nights. I struggled with what I heard in the meeting. I feel like I looked in the mirror, and what I saw concerned me."

The group seemed to relax as Mark talked of his uneasiness. When Mark was finished, Jan nodded and declared, "Exactly! Before the meeting I felt pretty good about our leadership performance. However, after listening to Wilma, I didn't feel as proud. I left the meeting knowing that I have been not been authentic. I have been 'naked.' I came away with the feeling that becoming authentic will not be easy. I thought about wearing my 'AM I

94

NAKED?' T-shirt, but I wasn't sure that I was ready. Mark, did you feel ready when you got dressed this morning?"

Mark kept smiling broadly. "Did I feel ready to wear the shirt? Heavens, no! How can you be ready to wear the shirt when you know the answer is going to be that you *are* naked? I left the meeting with clarity about that issue. I believe that I have not been authentic, but I have been hoping that no one would notice."

"Why did you wear the shirt?" Randy asked, trying to discern Mark's commitment to being different in the future.

Mark now stood up. He seemed ready to tell the Team what he was thinking. "I don't think that I have a choice. I must wear the shirt. I believe that once you realize you are acting 'inauthentically,' you don't have much of a choice."

"No choice?" Randy asked, still trying to understand Mark's feelings.

"Exactly," Mark continued. "It's just like the Emperor in the story. Once the child spoke up, he had to make a choice. He could admit that he was naked. He could ignore the feedback and continue to pretend that he was dressed. Or he could punish the person who dared call him on his duplicity. If we intend to create a great company, only one of those choices makes sense. We have to admit that we are naked. We have to ask others for their opinions. We have to listen to the answers without being defensive. And then we have to get better—quickly. To do anything else would be to bury our heads in the sand and pretend."

"You mean sort of like what we have been doing to date?" Jan asked, stating the obvious. The entire Team laughed nervously. They seemed to agree with Mark and seemed ready for change, but they were unsure of what to do next.

Hap, always the team builder, tried to strike a positive tone. "Let's not lose sight of all our accomplishments. I feel like we are beating ourselves up unnecessarily. We have to be careful not to over-react to the Cladcom meeting."

Mark reacted quickly to Hap's comments. "I don't think that we are overreacting to the meeting. I don't consider our conversation to be negative. To the contrary, I find this entire dialogue exciting. I have been thoughtful—but energized. I feel that for the first time in a while I'm learning as a leader. In fact, this weekend I wrote down a few of my key learnings from the past several weeks."

"Let's hear them," Jan said. The Team sensed that Mark was ready to explain how ServiceProne would be different in the future.

But unlike in the past, Mark did not intend to give the Team direction. Instead, he was more introspective as he talked about what he had learned and the challenges that lay ahead.

"I firmly believe that I need to get dressed. And I also believe that I need *new clothes*. I can't put on the same clothes that I wore yesterday and expect things to be different tomorrow. I titled my list 'The Leader's New Clothes,' and I called my learning 'truths' because I believe that they are important."

"Would those be 'Naked Truths'?" joked Randy.

"I like that—Naked Truths," Mark said. "So here they are—my Naked Truths. Tell me where you disagree." And with that, Mark read from his notes that he had made over the weekend.

"Naked Truth Number One is," he began, "*Perception is all there is. We are authentic only when people perceive we are who we claim to be.* We can know this only if we solicit feedback from our teams and if we hear that feedback without reacting defensively to what people tell us.

"Naked Truth Number Two seems obvious but is easy to forget. *The higher you go in the organization, the more 'out of touch' you become.* We used to call this getting 'mushroomed'—that is when you are kept in the dark and fed manure. Now that may be a bit extreme, but there is no doubt that the more senior you are, the harder it is for people to share their real feelings with you. If they admire you, they won't want to disappoint you. If they fear you, it gets worse.

"Naked Truth Number Three," Mark continued, "hit me like a ton of bricks over the weekend. *If you are not ready to act—don't ask!* When people tell you that you are not 'walking your talk,' it makes you uncomfortable. But maybe even more important, when you get feedback, you must be acutely aware that your reaction to that feedback will define you as a leader. Simply asking the question creates the expectation that you will listen and change.

"The more I thought about Naked Truth Number Four, the more important it became to me. I strongly believe that *when it comes to authenticity, even little things can mean a lot.* People note the performances we reward, the behavior we tolerate, the choices we make, the people we promote, and the way we spend our time. From what they observe, they infer our priorities. At times, they are moved by what we might consider the smallest gesture. They can't read our minds, so they watch our behavior and make sweeping assumptions about what we value—and what we don't.

"Naked Truth Number Five," Mark went on, speaking very slowly to emphasize his point, "*You are what you habitually do.* The harsh truth is that it may take only one inauthentic act to be perceived as inauthentic. Many months of consistent action are required to develop an authentic reputation. It may not be fair. It is just the way it is. What we do once in a while does not define us.

"And, finally, Naked Truth Number Six—*authenticity is a journey, not a destination.* At best, a leader is always in the process of becoming authentic. It is not something that we are. It is something that we work to be day in and day out. The most we can hope for is to be more authentic tomorrow than we were today. Perceived authenticity must be earned—and that is hard work."

"Wow!" Hap exclaimed as he finished writing down the last "truth." "You did have a busy weekend." The group was struck with the amount of thought Mark had given these issues.

The room got very quiet for a minute before Jan spoke up. "Mark, to say that I agree with your 'truths' is an understatement. What occurs to me is that we have talked about similar issues before, but, for some reason, we didn't commit to changing our behavior. I know we SAID we were committed. But, somehow, our commitment to our commitment was lacking."

The group chuckled uneasily as Jan continued. "I'd like to suggest one more Naked Truth that we must come to grips with if we hope to be an authentic leadership team."

"A Seventh Naked Truth?" Mark asked.

"Exactly!" Jan smiled, sensing Mark's interest. "I am suggesting that Naked Truth Number Seven be *what you tolerate, you teach.* If we tolerate inauthentic behavior, we teach people that that behavior is acceptable."

The group was touched by the seventh Naked Truth. It was clear that everyone agreed with the Naked Truth Jan had suggested. They all knew they had tolerated inauthentic behavior. The awkward silence in the room was interrupted by only the sound of Team members shifting in their chairs.

Mark broke the silence as he responded to Jan's comments. "Jan, that is a great Naked Truth! I have been guilty of tolerating inauthentic behavior. I have tolerated it from others. Worse yet, I tolerated it from myself. I agree with you, Jan, tolerance can teach the wrong message. If we decide to take this journey, we all have to be committed to holding each other accountable for not tolerating inauthentic behavior in this group, as well as the rest of the company."

Mark was energized as he continued. It was as if the "Truths" had set him free. His passion was obvious to all. "We have a decision to make! We have to decide how we intend to lead. Do we continue to lead as we have in the past, or do we commit ourselves to being authentic leaders?"

Mark paused for a moment and briefly looked at each member of the Team. "For me, the decision is clear. I want to help make ServiceProne a great company. I want to be an authentic leader! I want to get dressed!"

He paused again and then continued. "Our experiences of the last several weeks remind me of one of my favorite poems, 'The Man in the Mirror.' I have always kept a copy of this poem in my office, but until recently it had not called me to action. Today, the words are ringing in my ears:

You can fool the whole world down the pathway of years,
And get pats on the back as you pass,
But the final reward will be heartache and tears,
If you've cheated the man in the glass.

Mark's voice cracked as he finished the poem. He waited, and then he looked directly in the eyes of every member of the Team. As he spoke, his voice was quiet, but his mannerisms gave witness to his commitment.

"I've had my share of pats on the back, and I must admit, they felt great at the time. But it's clear that I want and need more—for all of us. I don't want to fool anyone anymore. I now know that I have cheated the man in the mirror, and I'm ready to be better. I need to be better. I want to experience what it feels like to be authentic. I need your help; I can't do it alone. Are you ready?"

As Mark finished speaking, he sat down in his chair. He realized that he had been talking for some time, and he wasn't sure how the Team would react. At first, they looked surprised by Mark's passion and commitment. But then, almost in unison, the Team stood and started applauding. All at once, it became clear to Mark that the Team had been waiting for the chance to be become authentic leaders. They wanted to do something special.

We are not sure that they lived happily ever after, but, for the first time, this group had a chance.

THE END

The Naked Truths

When it comes to authenticity:

Perception is all there is.

*The higher you go in the organization,
the more "out of touch" you become.*

If you are not ready to act—don't ask!

Even little things can mean a lot.

You are what you habitually do.

It is a journey, not a destination.

What you tolerate, you teach.

ACKNOWLEDGMENTS

In every project, there is one person who makes it happen — no matter how big the obstacles that stand in the way. *The Leader's New Clothes* simply would not have happened without Karl Meinhardt. It was his idea to use the story, and much of the insight and humor in this book were taken from his experiences as a CIO and a team leader. Thank you again, Karl, for giving me the opportunity to participate.

I'd also like to thank Madelyn Hammond, Mike Meinhardt, Sharon Thies, Deb DeMars, Harry Rhodes, Deborah Stephens, Tom Parker, and my dad, Joe Heil, for taking the time to give us guidance and support.

And then there is Wilma True — the type of leader I aspire to be. In my life, Wilma is also known as Pam Landwirth, Lisa Harper, Mike McCloskey, and Pat O'Donnell, to name just a few. The lessons they taught me fill every page.

The Naked Truth is that all of what I do is made possible because of the loving support of Carol, Michaela, and Ryan — the most authentic group I know!

— GARY HEIL

ACKNOWLEDGMENTS

I have been repeatedly surprised at the effort required to create and complete this book. When I reflect on the number of people whose opinions I requested, whose experiences I drew upon, and whose assistance I relied upon, I am amazed. It is my reality to know that without what each of these people offered, the end result would not have been what it is. Therefore, I thank the following people for their help, their support, their belief in me, and, most of all, for their participation in my life:

- My partner, Gary Heil, for his guidance, his candor, and the opportunity to be involved in such a wonderful experience.
- Terry Jenkins, for bringing the scenes in the book to life.
- Donna Tobias, for providing neverending support and encouragement, and for taking care of the zoo while I was away.
- Michael Meinhardt, for manning the crank to make sure the wheels kept turning.
- Neva Meinhardt, for providing me with a lifetime of education that I used to the fullest on this project.

ACKNOWLEDGMENTS

- Brian King, Evy Smith, and Mark Miller, for their feedback.
- The team members I have managed, who have provided me with concrete proof that leading authentically creates motivated and inspired teams.

And, last but not least, a special thanks to those people who requested that they remain unnamed because they work in environments where this kind of exposure could be career-shortening. You know who you are!

— KARL MEINHARDT

ABOUT THE AUTHORS

GARY HEIL is an author, educator, lawyer, consultant, and coach. For the last three decades, he has been an ardent student of the human side of organizations. He was a pioneer in the study of loyal customer relationships and how these relationships have been affected by employee motivation. He remains a vocal and passionate advocate for finding more effective ways to lead inspired teams.

Gary is the coauthor of *Leadership and the Customer Revolution, One Size Fits One: Building Relationships One Customer and One Employee at a Time, Maslow on Management, Revisiting the Human Side of Enterprise, For the Love of the Game: The Art of Leading an Inspired Team,* and *The Winning Coach.*

In addition, Gary is the cofounder of the webcast *Leadership Lessons from the Fast Lane,* and he has been a commentator on Australian and American radio and television.

He has also served as an examiner for the Malcolm Baldrige National Quality Award and as an advisor and director for a number of technology start-ups.

With over twenty-five years as a technology professional, KARL MEINHARDT has served as a consultant for many companies regarding information technology strategies and services. As a former CIO and founder of several start-up companies, he has a full understanding of information as a powerful source of service. Karl's expertise with turning knowledge into a strategic advantage has assisted many organizations and companies in their long-term service goals, while focusing on building agile and adept information technology teams.

Using his complete understanding of software development strategies and the importance of corporate culture, he has helped companies to build information technology teams who can produce quality products on relatively short time frames. He believes in building teams who are empowered to execute their area of expertise, thus enabling those teams to work and grow in an environment based on knowledge, trust, and ownership.

As a public speaker, Karl has the unique ability to present complex concepts to a wide range of audiences, making these concepts understandable and entertaining.

Karl is a graduate of California Polytechnic State University, San Luis Obispo. He holds a Summa Cum Laude Bachelor of Science degree in Applied Mathematics.

THE LEADER'S NEW CLOTHES

www.theleadersnewclothes.com

This book is based on our experiences and those of our friends, but we are dedicated to finding authentic leaders globally. Through writing this book, we realized that there are most certainly countless stories and experiences that you, the reader, may be able to share with us. That said, we have developed an online forum where you can share your thoughts with us and other leaders who dream of being clothed.

Visit www.theleadersnewclothes.com to

- Share your ideas with us
- Give us your feedback on *The Leader's New Clothes*
- Tell us the ways in which you became a more authentic leader and inspired your team
- Give us your vote for the most authentic leader and the least authentic leader in the universe

We hope you enjoyed the book and look forward to engaging with you online.

For further information, please e-mail us at
info@theleadersnewclothes.com or call 1-800-337-1747.

Produced by Wilsted & Taylor Publishing Services

COPYEDITING: CAROLINE ROBERTS

DESIGN AND COMPOSITION: JEFF CLARK

TEXT: ELECTRA

DISPLAY: TAGLIENTE

Printed by Data Reproductions Corporation